COMMUNITY · CONNECTIONS

?

WHAT SHOULD I DO?
IF THERE IS A FIRE

BY WIL MARA

CHERRY
LAKE
Publishing

Published in the United States of America by Cherry Lake Publishing
Ann Arbor, Michigan
www.cherrylakepublishing.com

Content Adviser: Karen Sheehan, MD, MPH, Children's Memorial Hospital, Chicago, Illinois

Photo Credits: Cover, ©Blend Images/Alamy; page 5, ©Ron Frank/Shutterstock, Inc.;
page 7, ©Hans295/Dreamstime.com; page 9, ©Gunter Marx/EV/Alamy; page 11,
©Fancy/Alamy; page 13, ©ambrozinio/Shutterstock, Inc.; page 15,
©Paskee/Shutterstock, Inc.; page 17, ©Ronald Caswell/Shutterstock, Inc.; page 19,
©Big Pants Production/Shutterstock, Inc.; page 21, ©iStockphoto/Edward Shaw.

LIBRARY OF CONGRESS CATALOGING-IN-PUBLICATION DATA
Mara, Wil.
  What should I do? If there is a fire/by Wil Mara.
    p. cm.—(Community connections)
  Includes bibliographical references and index.
  ISBN-13: 978-1-61080-053-2 (lib. bdg.)
  ISBN-10: 1-61080-053-2 (lib. bdg.)
  1. Fires—Safety measures—Juvenile literature. 2. Fire prevention—Juvenile literature.
I. Title. II. Title: If there is a fire. III. Series.
  TH9148.M265 2011
  613.6—dc22   2010052172

Cherry Lake Publishing would like to acknowledge the
work of The Partnership for 21st Century Skills. Please
visit *www.21stcenturyskills.org* for more information.

Printed in the United States of America
Corporate Graphics Inc.
July 2011
CLFA09

IF THERE IS A FIRE

CONTENTS

WHAT SHOULD I DO?

A HOUSE ON FIRE

What would it be like to be trapped in a house that is on fire? Can you imagine how scary that would be? A house can burn very fast. Would you know what to do if this happened to you?

Make sure your family has a plan for getting out quickly if there is a fire in your home.

5

THE DANGERS OF FIRE

Fire can cause painful burns. It also creates harmful smoke. Breathing in smoke will make you cough and become very sick. You could even die.

Smoke can be just as dangerous to you as the fire can.

Can you guess how most people get hurt during fires? Do you think it is from burns? It is not! People in fires usually get hurt from breathing too much smoke.

7

DON'T HIDE—GET OUTSIDE!

Do not hide if you get caught in a house fire. You should get outside as fast as you can. Use the nearest door or window if you are on the first floor.

Do not stop to take anything with you. Yell so other people in the house will hear you.

Do not use the elevator if there is a fire in an apartment building. Use the stairs or a fire escape.

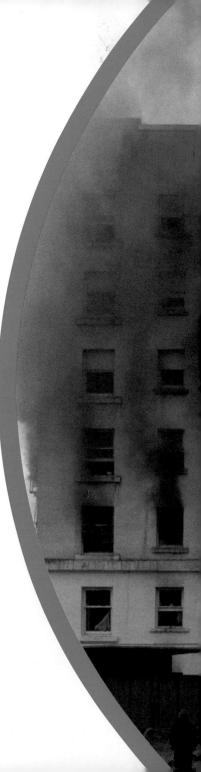

Touch all doors with the back of your hand before opening them. Do not open hot doors. There is probably fire on the other side.

Crawl on the floor if there is smoke in the air. There will be less smoke down low. Cover your mouth and nose. You can use a towel, a tissue, or your shirt.

Don't open a door if you see smoke coming from under it.

Apartment buildings should have a set of **fire stairs** on every floor. Get to these stairs if you can. Fires will not be able to burn there.

There should also be a **fire escape** outside one of your apartment windows. Go there if you cannot get to the fire stairs. Be very careful going down these steps.

Fire stairs have special doors to block fires.

Most apartment buildings have fire escape paths planned out. Ask the person in charge of your building about the plan. You should know it in case the building ever catches fire.

13

You might get trapped in a room where you cannot use the door or window to get out. Use a blanket or towel to cover the bottom of the door. This will keep smoke from getting in.

Open the window to get fresh air. Yell for help as loud as you can. Call **9-1-1** if you have a telephone.

Firefighters are trained to come to a burning house very quickly.

Do not go back in the house once you are outside. A burning house can fall down very easily. Instead, go to a neighbor's house and call 9-1-1.

Do not be scared of the **firefighters** when they come. They will help put out the fire. Do whatever they tell you to do.

Firefighters regularly check their fire hoses to be sure they will work properly when needed.

STOPPING FIRES BEFORE THEY START

The best way to fight a fire is to make sure it never starts. Never play with matches. Blow out candles before you go to bed. Do not leave towels or paper near a stove. Can you think of other fire dangers?

An electrical outlet with too many plugs is a very common fire hazard.

LOOK!

Walk around your house or apartment and look for fire dangers. Make a list and show it to your parents. They can help you get rid of these dangers.

19

Make sure your house has at least one **smoke detector** on each floor. Check that each smoke detector has working **batteries**.

Make an escape plan with your family in case a fire ever starts. Practice this plan until everyone can remember it. It will help you stay safe if there is a real fire!

Remind your parents to make sure your smoke detector has fresh batteries.

21

GLOSSARY

apartment buildings (uh-PAHRT-muhnt BIL-dingz) buildings divided into homes called apartments

batteries (BAT-ur-eez) small containers filled with chemicals that make electrical power

fire escape (FIRE i-SKAPE) a set of stairs on the outside of a building that can be used to get away from a fire

fire stairs (FIRE STAIRZ) a set of fireproof stairs on the inside of a building

firefighters (FIRE-fye-turz) workers who put out fires and rescue people caught in burning buildings

9-1-1 a special phone number you can call to get help during emergencies

smoke detector (SMOHK di-TEK-tur) a machine that makes noise when smoke or fire is near

FOR MORE INFORMATION

BOOKS

Barraclough, Sue. *Fire Safety*. Chicago: Heinemann Library, 2008.

Jacobs, Paula DuBois, and Jennifer Swender. *Fire Drill*. New York: Henry Holt, 2010.

Miller, Edward. *Fireboy to the Rescue! A Fire Safety Book*. New York: Holiday House, 2009.

WEB SITES

Sparky the Fire Dog
www.sparky.org/#/Sparky
Watch cartoons, read comics, and play games to learn more about fires.

USFA Kids
www.usfa.dhs.gov/kids/flash.shtm
Play fun games and learn about fire safety from the U.S. Fire Administration.

INDEX

ABOUT THE AUTHOR

Wil Mara is the award-winning author of more than 120 books, many of which are educational titles for children. More information about his work can be found at *www.wilmara.com.*

24